PRAISE FOR ~~POWER After~~ DV

Except for Becca, who is one of your amazing coaches in our programs, our clients' names have been changed to protect their identities.

"There is no other program like POWER After DV. This book should be the textbook for how to overcome the effects of domestic violence. Tina has such an amazing passion for helping women like me who have experienced domestic violence in past intimate relationships."

— *Steph*

"My experience with POWER After DV made me realize how much the negative words said to me as a child affected me and did not prepare me for success. Once I was able to change the narrative others wrote for me when I was young and discovered God's narrative, my life has totally changed."

— *Wendy*

"I really benefited from working through the masterclasses in the POWER After DV: Freedom from the Effects of Domestic Violence program. It gave me the confidence to move forward with stopping the abuse in my life. The course provided the framework I needed to heal and grow. Healing and hope poured forth as I completed each class."

— *Lisa*

"The weekly Sister Time was so very helpful. It was an integral component of this process. I was able to talk about and process my experiences. Receiving support at each point in this process allowed me to grow in courage. Upon completing the program, the strength I had allowed me to take the steps necessary to bring myself from fear to wholeness"

— *Terry*

"After an on-and-off relationship of five years bursting with domestic violence, God finally gave me enough courage and strength to leave. However, after leaving, I didn't realize that there was so much more that I needed to let God do to be free from the strongholds of domestic violence, and I honestly didn't even recognize what they truly were until I met Tina. She encouraged me to do her Proverbs 26 challenge. This challenge really touched on verbal abuse, how it no longer has power over you, and how to get freedom from that stronghold. It was very emotional and refreshing all at the same time, and during this, I started to change how I prayed, even how I talked, and I started taking control back over my life and the things that have been spoken over me and my life and my family's life. On the third day of doing the course and praying after each session, God delivered me right there in my mother's living room. That was the day I fully got freedom, and out of me came and went those nasty word curses that I let myself believe were true, that I let have power over my everyday life and mindsets. God gave me new mindsets and new words with purpose and life. He spoke over and into me that day. I would've even known those were there, and this wouldn't have happened if I hadn't taken this course. I am forever thankful for God using Tina this way because now I'm a free woman and mother. *I am free!*"

—*Becca*

POWER
after
DV
WORKBOOK

POWER

after

DV

WORKBOOK

TINA ANGELA LEE

For information on distribution rights, royalties, derivative works, or licensing opportunities on behalf of this content or work, please contact the publisher at the address below:

Farmhouse Publishings, LLC
P.O. Box 333
Spearfish, SD 57783

Although the author and publisher have tried to ensure that the information and advice in this book were correct and accurate at press time, the author and publisher do not assume and disclaim any liability to any party for any loss, damage, or disruption caused by acting upon the information in this book or by errors or omissions, whether such errors or omissions result from negligence, accident, or any other cause.

ISBN (Softcover): 979-8-9881344-5-9

Design by Heidi Caperton

Printed in the United States of America.

I dedicate this
journal to you,
my sweet sister.

POWER **AFTER DV:**

Freedom from the Effects of Domestic Violence

*P*owerful
*O*vercoming
*W*omen
*E*ngaging in
*R*estoration

To learn more about the
POWER After DV Christian Life Coaching program,
go to: www.purposeafterdv.com

TABLE OF CONTENTS

INTRODUCTION

Dear strong, beautiful, confident woman of God,

I am thrilled to walk alongside you on this transformative journey towards total freedom from the effects of domestic violence. Through the pages of this workbook, we will confront the painful shadows of your past, unveil the power and love of your heavenly Father, and emerge as overcomers, more radiant than ever.

Though challenging, each step of this process will lead to a profound sense of healing and liberation.

Together, we will delve into the depths of your experiences, understanding the intricate webs of abuse that have affected your life. Nevertheless, that is just the beginning. We will then take those shattered pieces, surrender them to God, and allow His grace to rebuild your spirit.

As we navigate through the different types of abuse, remember that you are not alone in this journey. Your heavenly Father is with you every step of the way, and your sisters in Christ stand beside you in solidarity and support. The trauma you bring to light is not a burden to carry; it is a stepping stone to ultimate victory.

This workbook is not merely a self-help tool, but a divine guide to your heart and soul. We will unlock the power of repentance and forgiveness, essential keys to releasing the past and embracing the bright future God has ordained for you.

So, with courage, faith, and a heart ready for transformation, let us begin this journey of renewal, redemption, and rediscovery. You are a strong, beautiful, confident woman of God, and your story is far from over. Together, we will ensure that the best chapters are yet to come.

Chapter 1

STRONG, BEAUTIFUL, CONFIDENT WOMAN OF GOD

I am a
Strong
Beautiful
Confident
Woman
Of God!

When you change your narrative and shed the labels of victim and survivor of domestic violence, you set yourself free from victimhood and release yourself to discover and walk in the fullness of the PURPOSE and plans that God has created for you to walk in...

The POWER of Words: There are two specific words that the domestic violence world has spoken over us and taught us to speak over ourselves.

VICTIM of Domestic Violence: What does the word victim mean to you?

_____

_____

_____

_____

_____

_____

SURVIVOR of Domestic Violence: What does the word survivor mean to you?

_____

_____

_____

_____

_____

_____

Repeat after me:

I am a Strong, Beautiful, Confident Woman of God!

The POWER of the WORD: Look up the following verses in your favorite version of the Bible and write them out.

Hebrews 4:12

_____

_____

_____

Psalm 107:20

_____

_____

_____

Psalm 119:105

_____

_____

_____

List some of the amazing qualities of the WORD of God:

_____

_____

_____

_____

_____

_____

_____

Chapter 2

TALK, ASK, LISTEN, RECORD: A DIVINE CONVERSATION

When you take the time to stop and listen, you can begin to hear God's voice speaking directly to your heart...

Spend some quiet time with the Lord and begin to practice **Talk, Ask, Listen, Record.**

Ask the Lord to tell you how He feels about this journey you are embarking on with Him.

_____

_____

_____

_____

_____

_____

_____

_____

_____

_____

_____

_____

_____

_____

Chapter 3

GETTING IT ALL OUT: THE FOUR-SQUARE ACTIVITY

When you recognize the full scope of domestic violence as well as the full impact it has had on your life, you can begin the healing process...

Square #1 What an ex-husband, boyfriend, or intimate partner has done to you.	Square #2 What other people (parents, teachers, friends, etc.) have done to you.
Square #3 What you have done to yourself.	Square #4 What you have done to others.

Spend some quiet time with the Lord and continue practicing **Talk, Ask, Listen, Record.**

Ask the Lord to tell you what His thoughts and feelings are for you personally as His daughter.

Chapter 4

GETTING FREE FROM IT ALL: THE FOUR-STEP FRAMEWORK TO FREEDOM

When you partner with God and allow Him to help you face the abuse in your life, you can truly get freedom from its effects...

The Four Step Framework to Freedom

Step #1 - POWER
Repentance & Forgiveness

Step #2 - PURPOSE
Restoration & Foundation

Step #3 - PATHWAY
Responsibility & Future

Step #4 - PASSION
Resources & Freedom

Spend some quiet time with the Lord and continue practicing **Talk, Ask, Listen, Record.**

Ask the Lord for His encouraging words to you as you get ready to face the abuse in your past.

_____

_____

_____

_____

_____

_____

_____

_____

_____

_____

_____

_____

_____

_____

_____

_____

_____

_____

_____

_____

Foundation Scriptures: Look up the following verses in your favorite version of the Bible and write them out. Before you begin moving through each type of abuse, ask the Lord to reveal what He wants you to know about each of our foundation scriptures.

Step 1 - Repentance and Forgiveness – POWER

Repentance: Acts 26:20

_____

_____

Ask the Lord to speak to you about the importance of repentance.

_____

_____

_____

_____

Forgiveness: Matthew 6:14-15

_____

_____

Ask the Lord to speak to you about the importance of forgiveness.

_____

_____

_____

_____

Foundation Scriptures: Look up the following verses in your favorite version of the Bible and write them out. Before you begin moving through each type of abuse, ask the Lord to reveal what He wants you to know about each of our foundation scriptures.

Step 2 - Restoration and Foundation – PURPOSE

Restoration: Jeremiah 30:3

_____

_____

Ask the Lord to speak to you about the importance of restoration.

_____

_____

_____

_____

Foundation: Matthew 7:24

_____

_____

Ask the Lord to speak to you about the importance of foundation.

_____

_____

_____

_____

Foundation Scriptures: Look up the following verses in your favorite version of the Bible and write them out. Before you begin moving through each type of abuse, ask the Lord to reveal what He wants you to know about each of our foundation scriptures.

Step 3 - Responsibility and Future – PATHWAY

Responsibility: Ezra 10:4

Ask the Lord to speak to you about the importance of responsibility.

Future: Jeremiah 29:11

Ask the Lord to speak to you about the importance of the future.

Foundation Scriptures: Look up the following verses in your favorite version of the Bible and write them out. Before you begin moving through each type of abuse, ask the Lord to reveal what He wants you to know about each of our foundation scriptures.

Step 4 - Resources and Freedom - PASSION

Resources: 2 Kings 4:2

_____

_____

Ask the Lord to speak to you about the importance of resources.

_____

_____

_____

_____

Freedom: Galatians 5:1

_____

_____

Ask the Lord to speak to you about the importance of the freedom.

_____

_____

_____

_____

Chapter 5

FREEDOM FROM THE EFFECTS OF VERBAL ABUSE

An undeserved curse will be powerless to harm you. It may flutter over you like a bird, but it will find no place to land.

—PROVERBS 26:2 (TPT)

When you recognize verbal abuse and identify how it has impacted your life, you can change your narrative by changing your mindset about your identity...

The Definition of Verbal Abuse: What does verbal abuse mean to you?

_____

_____

_____

_____

The Target of the Enemy – Your Identity

What are some ungodly beliefs you have believed about yourself?

_____

_____

_____

_____

The Effect on Our Life

How have these ungodly beliefs shaped your identity?

_____

_____

_____

_____

Recognizing Verbal Abuse: Write out some examples of verbal abuse from your life.

Name Calling:

_____

_____

_____

Condescension:

_____

_____

_____

Manipulation:

_____

_____

_____

Criticism:

_____

_____

_____

Demeaning Comments:

_____

_____

_____

Threats:

_____

_____

_____

Blame:

_____

_____

_____

Accusations:

_____

_____

_____

Withholding:

_____

_____

_____

Gaslighting:

_____

_____

_____

Circular Arguments:

_____

_____

_____

Bible Study: Look up **Proverbs 26:2** in your favorite version of the Bible and write it out.

_____

_____

_____

_____

_____

Talk, Ask, Listen, Record: Ask the Lord to speak to you about this verse.

_____

_____

_____

_____

_____

_____

_____

_____

_____

_____

The Four-Square Activity: Focusing on Square #1, answer the following questions to help you get freedom from the effects of verbal abuse from an intimate partner.

What has an ex-husband, boyfriend, or intimate partner spoken over you?

_____

_____

_____

_____

How have these words impacted your life?

_____

_____

_____

_____

What do you believe about yourself because of these words?

_____

_____

_____

_____

How can you change your narrative?

_____

_____

_____

_____

The Four-Square Activity: Focusing on Square #2, answer the following questions to help you get freedom from the effects of verbal abuse from other people.

What has a parent, teacher, friend, etc., spoken over you?

_____

_____

_____

_____

How have these words impacted your life?

_____

_____

_____

_____

What do you believe about yourself because of these words?

_____

_____

_____

_____

How can you change your narrative?

_____

_____

_____

_____

The Four-Square Activity: Focusing on Square #3, answer the following questions to help you get freedom from the effects of verbal abuse from yourself.

What have you spoken over yourself?

How have these words impacted your life?

What do you believe about yourself because of these words?

How can you change your narrative?

The Four-Square Activity: Focusing on Square #4, answer the following questions to help you get freedom from the effects of verbal abuse that you have done to others.

What have you spoken over others?

_____

_____

_____

_____

How have these words impacted the lives of others?

_____

_____

_____

_____

What do you believe about yourself because of the words you have spoken over others?

_____

_____

_____

_____

How can you change your narrative?

_____

_____

_____

_____

The Four-Step Framework to Freedom – Step 1 – Repentance:

Look up **Acts 26:20** in the Amplified version of the Bible and write it out.

_____

_____

_____

_____

Talk, Ask, Listen, Record: Ask the Lord to give you deeper revelation about this verse.

_____

_____

_____

_____

_____

_____

What do you need to repent for?

_____

_____

_____

_____

_____

The Four-Step Framework to Freedom – Step 1 – Forgiveness:

Look up **Matthew 6:14-15** in the Amplified version of the Bible and write it out.

_____

_____

_____

_____

Talk, Ask, Listen, Record: Ask the Lord to give you deeper revelation about this verse.

_____

_____

_____

_____

_____

_____

Who do you need to forgive or ask forgiveness from?

_____

_____

_____

_____

_____

POWER Strategy Mapping

While learning about verbal abuse, what was your biggest Ah-Ha moment?

_____

_____

_____

_____

When it comes to verbal abuse, where are you still stuck?

_____

_____

_____

_____

What was the biggest revelation God gave you about verbal abuse?

_____

_____

_____

_____

What are your goals and next best steps to overcome verbal abuse completely?

_____

_____

_____

_____

Chapter 6

FREEDOM FROM THE EFFECTS OF PHYSICAL ABUSE

When you recognize physical abuse and identify how it has impacted your life, you can change your narrative by changing your mindset about your physical safety...

The Definition of Physical Abuse: What does physical abuse mean to you?

_____

_____

_____

_____

_____

The Target of the Enemy – Your Sense of Physical Safety and Security

What are some ungodly beliefs you have believed about your physical safety and security?

_____

_____

_____

_____

The Effect on Our Life

How have these ungodly beliefs shaped your beliefs about your physical safety and security?

_____

_____

_____

_____

Recognizing Physical Abuse: Write out some examples of physical abuse from your life.

Abuse Involving Physical Contact:

_____

_____

_____

_____

_____

_____

Abuse Involving the Use of an Object:

_____

_____

_____

_____

_____

Abuse Involving the Use of Size or Presence:

_____

_____

_____

_____

_____

_____

Bible Study: Look up **2 Samuel 22:3** in your favorite version of the Bible and write it out.

_____

_____

_____

_____

Talk, Ask, Listen, Record: Ask the Lord to speak to you about this verse.

_____

_____

_____

_____

_____

_____

_____

_____

_____

_____

_____

_____

_____

_____

The Four-Square Activity: Focusing on Square #1, answer the following questions to help you get freedom from the effects of physical abuse from an intimate partner.

What has an ex-husband, boyfriend, or intimate partner done to you?

_____

_____

_____

_____

How have these actions impacted your life?

_____

_____

_____

_____

What do you believe about yourself because of these actions?

_____

_____

_____

_____

How can you change your narrative?

_____

_____

_____

_____

The Four-Square Activity: Focusing on Square #2, answer the following questions to help you get freedom from the effects of physical abuse from other people.

What has a parent, teacher, friend, etc., done to you?

_____

_____

_____

_____

How have these actions impacted your life?

_____

_____

_____

_____

What do you believe about yourself because of these actions?

_____

_____

_____

_____

How can you change your narrative?

_____

_____

_____

_____

The Four-Square Activity: Focusing on Square #3, answer the following questions to help you get freedom from the effects of physical abuse from yourself.

What have you done to yourself?

_____

_____

_____

_____

How have these actions impacted your life?

_____

_____

_____

_____

What do you believe about yourself because of these actions?

_____

_____

_____

_____

How can you change your narrative?

_____

_____

_____

_____

The Four-Square Activity: Focusing on Square #4, answer the following questions to help you get freedom from the effects of physical abuse that you have done to others.

What have you done to others?

_____

_____

_____

_____

How have these actions impacted the lives of others?

_____

_____

_____

_____

What do you believe about yourself because of these actions?

_____

_____

_____

_____

How can you change your narrative?

_____

_____

_____

_____

The Four-Step Framework to Freedom – Step 1 – Repentance:

Look up **Acts 26:20** in a third version of the Bible and write it out.

_____

_____

_____

_____

Talk, Ask, Listen, Record: Ask the Lord for deeper revelation about this verse.

_____

_____

_____

_____

_____

_____

_____

What do you need to repent for?

_____

_____

_____

_____

_____

The Four-Step Framework to Freedom – Step 1 – Forgiveness:

Look up **Matthew 6:14-15** in a third version of the Bible and write it out.

_____

_____

_____

_____

Talk, Ask, Listen, Record: Ask the Lord for deeper revelation about this verse.

_____

_____

_____

_____

_____

_____

_____

Who do you need to forgive or ask forgiveness from?

_____

_____

_____

_____

_____

_____

The Escalation of Violence Scale: Starting at the bottom of the scale, highlight "Relationship Begins," then go up the scale line by line and highlight every line reflecting what happened in your relationship.[1]

Death
Severe Injury
Injury with a weapon
Attempted Strangulation
Threatens with a weapon
Beats up: pinned down/repeated blows
Hits with an object or closed fist
Kicks, bites, punches, confines
Slaps with an open hand
Grabs, pushed, shoves or throws objects
Destroys property
Threatens to harm loved ones and/or pets
Coerces, threatens, intimidates
Name calling, insults, attacks self-esteem, critical of personality
Isolates/discourages relationships with family/friends
Purposely hurts feelings/withholds compassion
Accidentally hurts feelings of loved ones
Batterer is charming, loving and extremely attentive to partner's every need
Relationship begins

Write down your thoughts about this activity:

_____

_____

_____

_____

_____

_____

_____

_____

_____

---

1 "Turning Point Domestic Violence Services," Turningpoint, n.d., https://www.turningpointdv.org/.

POWER Strategy Mapping

While learning about physical abuse, what was your biggest Ah-Ha moment?

_____

_____

_____

_____

When it comes to physical abuse, where are you still stuck?

_____

_____

_____

_____

What was the biggest revelation God gave you about physical abuse?

_____

_____

_____

_____

What are your goals and next best steps to overcome physical abuse completely?

_____

_____

_____

_____

Chapter 7

FREEDOM FROM THE EFFECTS OF SEXUAL ABUSE

When you recognize sexual abuse and identify how it has impacted your life, you can change your narrative by changing your mindset about your identity as a woman...

The Definition of Sexual Abuse: What does sexual abuse mean to you?

The Target of the Enemy – Your Identity as a Woman

What are some ungodly beliefs you have believed about your identity as a woman?

The Effect on Our Life

How have these ungodly beliefs shaped your beliefs about your identity as a woman?

Recognizing Sexual Abuse: Write out some examples of sexual abuse from your life.

Types of Intimate Partner Sexual Violence:

_____

_____

_____

_____

Recognizing the Complexity of Defining Sexual Assault:

_____

_____

_____

_____

Longer Lasting Trauma within Intimate Relationships:

_____

_____

_____

_____

Advice to Endure Sexual Assault and Secondary Wounding:

_____

_____

_____

_____

Bible Study: Read **Acts 18** in your favorite version of the Bible.

Talk, Ask, Listen, Record: Ask the Lord to speak to you about Aquila and Priscilla's relationship.

_____

_____

_____

_____

_____

_____

_____

_____

_____

_____

_____

_____

_____

_____

_____

_____

_____

The Four-Square Activity: Focusing on Square #1, answer the following questions to help you get freedom from the effects of sexual abuse from an intimate partner.

What has an ex-husband, boyfriend, or intimate partner done to you?

_____

_____

_____

_____

How have these actions impacted your life?

_____

_____

_____

What do you believe about yourself because of these actions?

_____

_____

_____

How can you change your narrative?

_____

_____

_____

The Four-Square Activity: Focusing on Square #2, answer the following questions to help you get freedom from the effects of sexual abuse from other people.

What has a parent, teacher, friend, etc., done to you?

_____

_____

_____

_____

How have these actions impacted your life?

_____

_____

_____

_____

What do you believe about yourself because of these actions?

_____

_____

_____

_____

How can you change your narrative?

_____

_____

_____

_____

The Four-Square Activity: Focusing on Square #3, answer the following questions to help you get freedom from the effects of sexual abuse from yourself.

What have you done to yourself?

_____

_____

_____

_____

How have these actions impacted your life?

_____

_____

_____

_____

What do you believe about yourself because of these actions?

_____

_____

_____

_____

How can you change your narrative?

_____

_____

_____

_____

The Four-Square Activity: Focusing on Square #4, answer the following questions to help you get freedom from the effects of sexual abuse that you have done to others.

What have you done to others?

_____

_____

_____

_____

How have these actions impacted the lives of others?

_____

_____

_____

What do you believe about yourself because of these actions?

_____

_____

_____

How can you change your narrative?

_____

_____

_____

_____

The Four-Step Framework to Freedom – Step 1 – Repentance:

Remembering our foundation verse, **Acts 26:20** - What do you need to repent for?

_____

_____

_____

_____

_____

_____

_____

_____

The Four-Step Framework to Freedom – Step 1 – Forgiveness:

Remembering our foundation verse **Matthew 6:14-15** - Who do you need to forgive or ask forgiveness from?

_____

_____

_____

_____

_____

_____

_____

POWER Strategy Mapping

While learning about sexual abuse, what was your biggest Ah-Ha moment?

_____

_____

_____

_____

When it comes to sexual abuse, where are you still stuck?

_____

_____

_____

_____

What was the biggest revelation God gave you about sexual abuse?

_____

_____

_____

_____

What are your goals and next best steps to overcome sexual abuse completely?

_____

_____

_____

_____

Chapter 8

FREEDOM FROM THE EFFECTS OF EMOTIONAL ABUSE

When you recognize emotional abuse and identify how it has impacted your life, you can change your narrative by changing your mindset about how you feel about yourself and the world around you...

The Definition of Emotional Abuse: What does emotional abuse mean to you?

_____

_____

_____

_____

The Target of the Enemy – Your Heart

What are some ungodly beliefs you have believed about how you feel about yourself?

_____

_____

_____

The Effect on Our Life

How have these ungodly beliefs shaped how you feel about yourself?

_____

_____

_____

Recognizing Emotional Abuse: Write out some examples of emotional abuse from your life.

Humiliation, Negating, and Constant Criticism:

Control and Shame:

Accusing, Blaming and Denial:

Emotional Neglect and Isolation:

Bible Study: Look up **1 Corinthians 1:8** in your favorite version of the Bible and write it out.

Talk, Ask, Listen, Record: Ask the Lord to speak to you about this verse.

Bible Study: Look up **Romans 8:37** in your favorite version of the Bible and write it out.

_____

_____

_____

_____

Talk, Ask, Listen, Record: Ask the Lord to speak to you about this verse.

_____

_____

_____

_____

_____

_____

_____

_____

_____

_____

_____

_____

_____

The Four-Square Activity: Focusing on Square #1, answer the following questions to help you get freedom from the effects of emotional abuse from an intimate partner.

What has an ex-husband, boyfriend, or intimate partner done to you?

_____

_____

_____

_____

How have these actions impacted your life?

_____

_____

_____

_____

What do you believe about yourself because of these actions?

_____

_____

_____

_____

How can you change your narrative?

_____

_____

_____

_____

The Four-Square Activity: Focusing on Square #2, answer the following questions to help you get freedom from the effects of emotional abuse from other people.

What has a parent, teacher, friend, etc., done to you?

_____

_____

_____

_____

How have these actions impacted your life?

_____

_____

_____

What do you believe about yourself because of these actions?

_____

_____

_____

How can you change your narrative?

_____

_____

_____

_____

The Four-Square Activity: Focusing on Square #3, answer the following questions to help you get freedom from the effects of emotional abuse from yourself.

What have you done to yourself?

_____

_____

_____

_____

How have these actions impacted your life?

_____

_____

_____

_____

What do you believe about yourself because of these actions?

_____

_____

_____

_____

How can you change your narrative?

_____

_____

_____

_____

The Four-Square Activity: Focusing on Square #4, answer the following questions to help you get freedom from the effects of emotional abuse that you have done to others.

What have you done to others?

_____

_____

_____

_____

How have these actions impacted the lives of others?

_____

_____

_____

_____

What do you believe about yourself because of these actions?

_____

_____

_____

_____

How can you change your narrative?

_____

_____

_____

_____

The Four-Step Framework to Freedom – Step 1 – Repentance:

Remembering our foundation verse, **Acts 26:20** - What do you need to repent for?

_____

_____

_____

_____

_____

_____

_____

The Four-Step Framework to Freedom – Step 1 – Forgiveness:

Remembering our foundation verse **Matthew 6:14-15** - Who do you need to forgive or ask forgiveness from?

_____

_____

_____

_____

_____

_____

_____

POWER Strategy Mapping

While learning about emotional abuse, what was your biggest Ah-Ha moment?

When it comes to emotional abuse, where are you still stuck?

What was the biggest revelation God gave you about emotional abuse?

What are your goals and next best steps to overcome emotional abuse completely?

Chapter 9

FREEDOM FROM THE EFFECTS OF PSYCHOLOGICAL ABUSE

When you recognize psychological abuse and identify how it has impacted your life, you can change your narrative by changing your mindset about what you think about yourself and the world around you...

The Definition of Psychological Abuse: What does psychological abuse mean to you?

_____

_____

_____

_____

_____

The Target of the Enemy – Your Mind

What are some ungodly beliefs you have believed about how you think about yourself?

_____

_____

_____

_____

The Effect on Our Life

How have these ungodly beliefs shaped how you think about yourself?

_____

_____

_____

_____

Recognizing Psychological Abuse: Write out some examples of psychological abuse from your life.

Psychological vs. Emotional Abuse:

_____

_____

_____

_____

Lingering Trauma:

_____

_____

_____

_____

More examples from my life:

_____

_____

_____

_____

_____

_____

_____

_____

Bible Study: Read **1 Samuel 25** in your favorite version of the Bible.

Talk, Ask, Listen, Record: Ask the Lord to speak to you about Abigail's story.

The Four-Square Activity: Focusing on Square #1, answer the following questions to help you get freedom from the effects of psychological abuse from an intimate partner.

What has an ex-husband, boyfriend, or intimate partner done to you?

_____

_____

_____

_____

How have these actions impacted your life?

_____

_____

_____

_____

What do you believe about yourself because of these actions?

_____

_____

_____

_____

How can you change your narrative?

_____

_____

_____

_____

The Four-Square Activity: Focusing on Square #2, answer the following questions to help you get freedom from the effects of psychological abuse from other people.

What has a parent, teacher, friend, etc., done to you?

_____

_____

_____

_____

How have these actions impacted your life?

_____

_____

_____

_____

What do you believe about yourself because of these actions?

_____

_____

_____

_____

How can you change your narrative?

_____

_____

_____

_____

The Four-Square Activity: Focusing on Square #3, answer the following questions to help you get freedom from the effects of psychological abuse from yourself.

What have you done to yourself?

_____

_____

_____

_____

How have these actions impacted your life?

_____

_____

_____

_____

What do you believe about yourself because of these actions?

_____

_____

_____

_____

How can you change your narrative?

_____

_____

_____

_____

The Four-Square Activity: Focusing on Square #4, answer the following questions to help you get freedom from the effects of psychological abuse that you have done to others.

What have you done to others?

_____

_____

_____

_____

How have these actions impacted the lives of others?

_____

_____

_____

_____

What do you believe about yourself because of these actions?

_____

_____

_____

_____

How can you change your narrative?

_____

_____

_____

_____

The Four-Step Framework to Freedom – Step 1 – Repentance:

Remembering our foundation verse, **Acts 26:20** - What do you need to repent for?

_____

_____

_____

_____

_____

_____

_____

The Four-Step Framework to Freedom – Step 1 – Forgiveness:

Remembering our foundation verse **Matthew 6:14-15** - Who do you need to forgive or ask forgiveness from?

_____

_____

_____

_____

_____

_____

POWER Strategy Mapping

While learning about psychological abuse, what was your biggest Ah-Ha moment?

_____

_____

_____

_____

When it comes to psychological abuse, where are you still stuck?

_____

_____

_____

_____

What was the biggest revelation God gave you about psychological abuse?

_____

_____

_____

_____

What are your goals and next best steps to overcome psychological abuse completely?

_____

_____

_____

_____

Chapter 10

FREEDOM FROM THE EFFECTS OF FINANCIAL ABUSE

When you recognize financial abuse and identify how it has impacted your life, you can change your narrative by changing your mindset about money...

The Definition of Financial Abuse: What does financial abuse mean to you?

_____

_____

_____

_____

_____

The Target of the Enemy – Your Financial Security

What are some ungodly beliefs you have believed about money?

_____

_____

_____

_____

_____

The Effect on Our Life

How have these ungodly beliefs shaped your beliefs about money?

_____

_____

_____

_____

_____

Recognizing Financial Abuse: Write out some examples of financial abuse from your life.

Exploiting Your Resources:

_____

_____

_____

_____

It's not just about money; it's about power and control:

_____

_____

_____

_____

Interfering With Your Job:

_____

_____

_____

_____

Controlling Shared Assets and Resources:

_____

_____

_____

_____

Bible Study: Look up **Matthew 6:25-34** in your favorite version of the Bible.

Talk, Ask, Listen, Record: Ask the Lord to speak to you about this passage.

_____

_____

_____

_____

_____

_____

_____

_____

_____

_____

_____

_____

_____

_____

_____

_____

_____

_____

The Four-Square Activity: Focusing on Square #1, answer the following questions to help you get freedom from the effects of financial abuse from an intimate partner.

What has an ex-husband, boyfriend, or intimate partner done to you?

_____

_____

_____

_____

How have these actions impacted your life?

_____

_____

_____

What do you believe about yourself because of these actions?

_____

_____

_____

How can you change your narrative?

_____

_____

_____

_____

The Four-Square Activity: Focusing on Square #2, answer the following questions to help you get freedom from the effects of financial abuse from other people.

What has a parent, teacher, friend, etc., done to you?

_____

_____

_____

_____

How have these actions impacted your life?

_____

_____

_____

_____

What do you believe about yourself because of these actions?

_____

_____

_____

_____

How can you change your narrative?

_____

_____

_____

_____

The Four-Square Activity: Focusing on Square #3, answer the following questions to help you get freedom from the effects of financial abuse from yourself.

What have you done to yourself?

_____

_____

_____

_____

How have these actions impacted your life?

_____

_____

_____

_____

What do you believe about yourself because of these actions?

_____

_____

_____

_____

How can you change your narrative?

_____

_____

_____

_____

The Four-Square Activity: Focusing on Square #4, answer the following questions to help you get freedom from the effects of financial abuse that you have done to others.

What have you done to others?

_____

_____

_____

_____

How have these actions impacted the lives of others?

_____

_____

_____

_____

What do you believe about yourself because of these actions?

_____

_____

_____

_____

How can you change your narrative?

_____

_____

_____

_____

The Four-Step Framework to Freedom – Step 1 – Repentance:

Remembering our foundation verse, **Acts 26:20** - What do you need to repent for?

_____

_____

_____

_____

_____

_____

_____

_____

_____

The Four-Step Framework to Freedom – Step 1 – Forgiveness:

Remembering our foundation verse **Matthew 6:14-15** - Who do you need to forgive or ask forgiveness from?

_____

_____

_____

_____

_____

_____

_____

_____

POWER Strategy Mapping

While learning about financial abuse, what was your biggest Ah-Ha moment?

_____

_____

_____

_____

When it comes to financial abuse, where are you still stuck?

_____

_____

_____

_____

What was the biggest revelation God gave you about financial abuse?

_____

_____

_____

_____

What are your goals and next best steps to overcome financial abuse completely?

_____

_____

_____

_____

Chapter 11

FREEDOM FROM THE EFFECTS OF LEGAL ABUSE

When you recognize legal abuse and identify how it has impacted your life, you can change your narrative by changing your mindset about authority figures...

The Definition of Legal Abuse: What does legal abuse mean to you?

_____

_____

_____

_____

_____

The Target of the Enemy – Your Sense of Justice

What are some ungodly beliefs you have believed about authority figures?

_____

_____

_____

_____

_____

The Effect on Our Life

How have these ungodly beliefs shaped your beliefs about authority figures?

_____

_____

_____

_____

_____

Recognizing Legal Abuse: Write some examples of legal abuse from your life.

Examples of Legal Abuse:

_____

_____

_____

_____

_____

_____

Gender-Driven Legal Abuse:

_____

_____

_____

_____

_____

_____

Jurisprudence-Driven Legal Abuse:

_____

_____

_____

_____

_____

_____

Bible Study: Look up **Proverbs 31:8-9** in your favorite version of the Bible.

Talk, Ask, Listen, Record: Ask the Lord to speak to you about these verses.

_____

_____

_____

_____

_____

_____

_____

Look up **Psalm 82:1-4** in your favorite version of the Bible.

Talk, Ask, Listen, Record: Ask the Lord to speak to you about these verses.

_____

_____

_____

_____

_____

_____

_____

The Four-Square Activity: Focusing on Square #1, answer the following questions to help you get freedom from the effects of legal abuse from an intimate partner.

What has an ex-husband, boyfriend, or intimate partner done to you?

_____

_____

_____

_____

How have these actions impacted your life?

_____

_____

_____

_____

What do you believe about yourself because of these actions?

_____

_____

_____

_____

How can you change your narrative?

_____

_____

_____

_____

The Four-Square Activity: Focusing on Square #2, answer the following questions to help you get freedom from the effects of legal abuse from other people.

What has a parent, teacher, friend, etc., done to you?

_____

_____

_____

_____

How have these actions impacted your life?

_____

_____

_____

_____

What do you believe about yourself because of these actions?

_____

_____

_____

_____

How can you change your narrative?

_____

_____

_____

_____

The Four-Square Activity: Focusing on Square #3, answer the following questions to help you get freedom from the effects of legal abuse from yourself.

What have you done to yourself?

_____

_____

_____

_____

How have these actions impacted your life?

_____

_____

_____

_____

What do you believe about yourself because of these actions?

_____

_____

_____

_____

How can you change your narrative?

_____

_____

_____

_____

The Four-Square Activity: Focusing on Square #4, answer the following questions to help you get freedom from the effects of legal abuse that you have done to others.

What have you done to others?

_____

_____

_____

_____

How have these actions impacted the lives of others?

_____

_____

_____

_____

What do you believe about yourself because of these actions?

_____

_____

_____

_____

How can you change your narrative?

_____

_____

_____

_____

The Four-Step Framework to Freedom – Step 1 – Repentance:

Remembering our foundation verse, **Acts 26:20** - What do you need to repent for?

_____

_____

_____

_____

_____

_____

_____

The Four-Step Framework to Freedom – Step 1 – Forgiveness:

Remembering our foundation verse **Matthew 6:14-15** - Who do you need to forgive or ask forgiveness from?

_____

_____

_____

_____

_____

_____

_____

POWER Strategy Mapping

While learning about legal abuse, what was your biggest Ah-Ha moment?

When it comes to legal abuse, where are you still stuck?

What was the biggest revelation God gave you about legal abuse?

What are your goals and next best steps to overcome legal abuse completely?

Chapter 12

FREEDOM FROM THE EFFECTS OF TECHNOLOGY ABUSE

When you recognize technology abuse and identify how it has impacted your life, you can change your narrative by changing your mindset about your privacy...

The Definition of Technology Abuse: What does technology abuse mean to you?

_____

_____

_____

_____

_____

The Target of the Enemy – Your Privacy

What are some ungodly beliefs you have believed about your privacy?

_____

_____

_____

_____

_____

The Effect on Our Life

How have these ungodly beliefs shaped your beliefs about your privacy?

_____

_____

_____

_____

_____

Recognizing Technology Abuse: Write down examples of technology abuse from your life.

Surreptitious Surveillance:

_____

_____

_____

Impersonation and Manipulation:

_____

_____

_____

Coercion Through Compromised Devices:

_____

_____

_____

Continuous Survelllance and Control:

_____

_____

_____

The Fear of Smart Homes:

_____

_____

_____

Bible Study: Look up **2 Timothy 1:7** in your favorite version of the Bible and write it out.

_____

_____

_____

_____

Talk, Ask, Listen, Record: Ask the Lord to speak to you about this verse.

_____

_____

_____

_____

_____

_____

_____

_____

_____

_____

_____

_____

_____

_____

The Four-Square Activity: Focusing on Square #1, answer the following questions to help you get freedom from the effects of technology abuse from an intimate partner.

What has an ex-husband, boyfriend, or intimate partner done to you?

_____

_____

_____

_____

How have these actions impacted your life?

_____

_____

_____

_____

What do you believe about yourself because of these actions?

_____

_____

_____

_____

How can you change your narrative?

_____

_____

_____

_____

The Four-Square Activity: Focusing on Square #2, answer the following questions to help you get freedom from the effects of technology abuse from other people.

What has a parent, teacher, friend, etc., done to you?

_____

_____

_____

_____

How have these actions impacted your life?

_____

_____

_____

_____

What do you believe about yourself because of these actions?

_____

_____

_____

_____

How can you change your narrative?

_____

_____

_____

_____

The Four-Square Activity: Focusing on Square #3, answer the following questions to help you get freedom from the effects of technology abuse from yourself.

What have you done to yourself?

How have these actions impacted your life?

What do you believe about yourself because of these actions?

How can you change your narrative?

The Four-Square Activity: Focusing on Square #4, answer the following questions to help you get freedom from the effects of technology abuse that you have done to others.

What have you done to others?

_____

_____

_____

_____

How have these actions impacted the lives of others?

_____

_____

_____

_____

What do you believe about yourself because of these actions?

_____

_____

_____

_____

How can you change your narrative?

_____

_____

_____

_____

The Four-Step Framework to Freedom – Step 1 – Repentance:

Remembering our foundation verse, **Acts 26:20** - What do you need to repent for?

_____

_____

_____

_____

_____

_____

_____

_____

The Four-Step Framework to Freedom – Step 1 – Forgiveness:

Remembering our foundation verse **Matthew 6:14-15** - Who do you need to forgive or ask forgiveness from?

_____

_____

_____

_____

_____

_____

_____

POWER Strategy Mapping

While learning about technology abuse, what was your biggest Ah-Ha moment?

_____

_____

_____

_____

When it comes to technology abuse, where are you still stuck?

_____

_____

_____

_____

What was the biggest revelation God gave you about technology abuse?

_____

_____

_____

_____

What are your goals and next best steps to overcome technology abuse completely?

_____

_____

_____

_____

Chapter 13

FREEDOM FROM THE EFFECTS OF SPIRITUAL ABUSE

When you recognize spiritual abuse and identify how it has impacted your life, you can change your narrative by changing your mindset about your PURPOSE...

The Definition of Spiritual Abuse: What does spiritual abuse mean to you?

_____

_____

_____

_____

_____

The Target of the Enemy – Your PURPOSE

What are some ungodly beliefs you have believed about your PURPOSE?

_____

_____

_____

_____

_____

The Effect on Our Life

How have these ungodly beliefs shaped your beliefs about your PURPOSE?

_____

_____

_____

_____

_____

Recognizing Spiritual Abuse: Write out some examples of spiritual abuse from your life.

Spiritual Authority to Maintain Dominance:

_____

_____

_____

_____

Censorship of Decision-Making:

_____

_____

_____

_____

Twisting Scripture:

_____

_____

_____

_____

Forced Submission:

_____

_____

_____

_____

Bible Study: Look up **Ephesians 5:22** in your favorite version of the Bible and write it out.

Talk, Ask, Listen, Record: Ask the Lord to speak to you about submission.

Bible Study: Look up **Colossians 3:19** in your favorite version of the Bible and write it out.

_____

_____

_____

_____

Talk, Ask, Listen, Record: Ask the Lord to speak to you about this verse.

_____

_____

_____

_____

_____

_____

_____

_____

_____

_____

_____

_____

_____

_____

The Four-Square Activity: Focusing on Square #1, answer the following questions to help you get freedom from the effects of spiritual abuse from an intimate partner.

What has an ex-husband, boyfriend, or intimate partner done to you?

_____

_____

_____

_____

How have these actions impacted your life?

_____

_____

_____

_____

What do you believe about yourself because of these actions?

_____

_____

_____

_____

How can you change your narrative?

_____

_____

_____

_____

The Four-Square Activity: Focusing on Square #2, answer the following questions to help you get freedom from the effects of spiritual abuse from other people.

What has a parent, teacher, friend, etc., done to you?

_____

_____

_____

_____

How have these actions impacted your life?

_____

_____

_____

What do you believe about yourself because of these actions?

_____

_____

_____

How can you change your narrative?

_____

_____

_____

_____

The Four-Square Activity: Focusing on Square #3, answer the following questions to help you get freedom from the effects of spiritual abuse from yourself.

What have you done to yourself?

_____

_____

_____

_____

How have these actions impacted your life?

_____

_____

_____

_____

What do you believe about yourself because of these actions?

_____

_____

_____

_____

How can you change your narrative?

_____

_____

_____

_____

The Four-Square Activity: Focusing on Square #4, answer the following questions to help you get freedom from the effects of spiritual abuse that you have done to others.

What have you done to others?

_____

_____

_____

_____

How have these actions impacted the lives of others?

_____

_____

_____

_____

What do you believe about yourself because of these actions?

_____

_____

_____

_____

How can you change your narrative?

_____

_____

_____

_____

The Four-Step Framework to Freedom – Step 1 – Repentance:

Remembering our foundation verse, **Acts 26:20** - What do you need to repent for?

_____

_____

_____

_____

_____

_____

_____

_____

The Four-Step Framework to Freedom – Step 1 – Forgiveness:

Remembering our foundation verse **Matthew 6:14-15** - Who do you need to forgive or ask forgiveness from?

_____

_____

_____

_____

_____

_____

_____

_____

POWER Strategy Mapping

While learning about spiritual abuse, what was your biggest Ah-Ha moment?

When it comes to spiritual abuse, where are you still stuck?

What was the biggest revelation God gave you about spiritual abuse?

What are your goals and next best steps to overcome spiritual abuse completely?

Chapter 14

FREEDOM FROM THE EFFECTS OF POST-SEPARATION ABUSE

When you recognize post-separation abuse and identify how it has impacted your life, you can change your narrative by changing your mindset about your autonomy...

The Definition of Post-Separation Abuse: What does post-separation abuse mean to you?

_____

_____

_____

_____

_____

The Target of the Enemy – Your Autonomy

What are some ungodly beliefs you have believed about your autonomy?

_____

_____

_____

_____

The Effect on Our Life

How have these ungodly beliefs shaped your beliefs about your autonomy?

_____

_____

_____

_____

Recognizing Post-Separation Abuse: Write out some examples of post-separation abuse from your life.

Alienation Allegations:

_____

_____

_____

_____

Neglectful or Abusive Parenting:

_____

_____

_____

_____

Discarding the Children:

_____

_____

_____

_____

Isolation:

_____

_____

_____

_____

Harassment and Stalking:

_____

_____

_____

_____

Legal Abuse:

_____

_____

_____

_____

Financial Abuse:

_____

_____

_____

_____

Counter Parenting:

_____

_____

_____

_____

Bible Study: Look up **Isaiah 30:1** in your favorite version of the Bible and write it out.

_____

_____

_____

_____

Talk, Ask, Listen, Record: Ask the Lord to speak to you about this verse.

_____

_____

_____

_____

_____

_____

_____

_____

_____

_____

_____

_____

_____

_____

The Four-Square Activity: Focusing on Square #1, answer the following questions to help you get freedom from the effects of post-separation abuse from an intimate partner.

What has an ex-husband, boyfriend, or intimate partner done to you?

_____

_____

_____

_____

How have these actions impacted your life?

_____

_____

_____

_____

What do you believe about yourself because of these actions?

_____

_____

_____

_____

How can you change your narrative?

_____

_____

_____

_____

The Four-Square Activity: Focusing on Square #2, answer the following questions to help you get freedom from the effects of post-separation abuse from other people.

What has a parent, teacher, friend, etc., done to you?

_____

_____

_____

_____

How have these actions impacted your life?

_____

_____

_____

_____

What do you believe about yourself because of these actions?

_____

_____

_____

_____

How can you change your narrative?

_____

_____

_____

_____

The Four-Square Activity: Focusing on Square #3, answer the following questions to help you get freedom from the effects of post-separation abuse from yourself.

What have you done to yourself?

_____

_____

_____

_____

How have these actions impacted your life?

_____

_____

_____

_____

What do you believe about yourself because of these actions?

_____

_____

_____

_____

How can you change your narrative?

_____

_____

_____

_____

The Four-Square Activity: Focusing on Square #4, answer the following questions to help you get freedom from the effects of post-separation abuse that you have done to others.

What have you done to others?

_____

_____

_____

_____

How have these actions impacted the lives of others?

_____

_____

_____

_____

What do you believe about yourself because of these actions?

_____

_____

_____

_____

How can you change your narrative?

_____

_____

_____

_____

The Four-Step Framework to Freedom – Step 1 – Repentance:

Remembering our foundation verse, **Acts 26:20** - What do you need to repent for?

_____

_____

_____

_____

_____

_____

_____

_____

The Four-Step Framework to Freedom – Step 1 – Forgiveness:

Remembering our foundation verse **Matthew 6:14-15** - Who do you need to forgive or ask forgiveness from?

_____

_____

_____

_____

_____

_____

_____

_____

POWER Strategy Mapping

While learning about post-separation abuse, what was your biggest Ah-Ha moment?

_____

_____

_____

_____

When it comes to post-separation abuse, where are you still stuck?

_____

_____

_____

_____

What was the biggest revelation God gave you about post-separation abuse?

_____

_____

_____

_____

What are your goals and next best steps to overcome post-separation abuse completely?

_____

_____

_____

_____

Chapter 15

YOU TRULY ARE A STRONG, BEAUTIFUL, CONFIDENT WOMAN OF GOD

The Victim to Victory Scale: Starting at the bottom of the scale, highlight "Abusive Relationship Ends," then go up the scale line by line and highlight every line reflecting what has happened since your relationship ended.

Abundant Life
Mess into Message…
Able to enjoy healthy relationships
Implements plan to better future
Considers school/career options
Repairs relationships with family/friends
Repairs relationships with children
Builds new friendships
Seeks counseling/support group
Recognizes a need for change
Swears off intimate relationships for good
Low income job/dependency on the system
Survival mode – just getting through the day
Angry at the world/feels like the world owes you
New destructive relationships
Unable to move beyond the abuse
Stuck in fear and hopelessness
Feelings of betrayal, anger and grief
Abusive Relationship Ends

Journal your thoughts about this activity:

_____

_____

_____

_____

_____

_____

_____

POWER Strategy Mapping:

What is your #1 goal to completely overcome the effects of DV and walk in victory?

_____

_____

_____

_____

What is the best thing you learned about yourself?

_____

_____

_____

_____

Complete this sentence...I am a:

_____

_____

_____

_____

How do you feel about your experience during POWER After DV:

_____

_____

_____

_____

PURPOSE = Pursuing Understanding and Revelation about our
Purpose through Opportunities, Skills, and Education

Ask the Lord to speak to you about PURPOSE After DV:

_____

_____

_____

_____

_____

_____

_____

_____

_____

_____

_____

_____

_____

After completing POWER After DV, what is your next best step?

_____

_____

_____

_____

_____

Woe to the rebellious children. This is the Lord's declaration, "They carry out a plan, but not mine. They make an alliance, but against my will, piling sin on top of sin."

—ISAIAH 30:1 (HCSB)

ABOUT THE AUTHOR

Tina Angela Lee, a seasoned advocate for women's empowerment, brings a wealth of knowledge to *POWER After DV: Freedom from the Effects of Domestic Violence.* With a background in education, advocacy, law, and theological studies and a passion for helping women gain freedom from the effects of domestic violence and walking out their God-given PURPOSE in life, Tina has dedicated her career to teaching, legal advocacy and spiritual guidance. Her commitment to fostering strength and resilience in the face of adversity shines through in this transformative guide. Tina holds a law degree and serves on the Survivor's Advisory Board for the Indiana Coalition Against Domestic Violence. She is committed to supporting women on their journey to freedom, healing, and PURPOSE

Tina is a passionate advocate for women who have experienced domestic violence and shares her own personal journey on the PURPOSE After Domestic Violence Podcast. Through powerful storytelling and insightful revelations, she sheds light on the impact of domestic violence and offers support, guidance, and hope to listeners. Tune in to this empowering podcast to gain a deeper understanding of the issue and discover resources for healing and moving forward.

The *POWER After DV: Freedom from the Effects of Domestic Violence* book takes you on a transformative journey through the nuanced layers of abuse—from the overt to the covert. Offering a unique blend of defining abuse, personal narratives, biblical insights, and practical strategies, this book sheds light on often-overlooked forms of abuse, with a focus on reclaiming your voice and changing the narrative of your life, guiding you from victimhood and just simply surviving to becoming a strong, beautiful, confident woman of God.

The POWER After DV Program is another valuable resource that provides masterclass videos, weekly Sister Time meetings, and a community of women on this journey with you. You don't have to walk alone, we are here to hold your hand and encourage you along the way.

If you have been blessed by this workbook, please share the message with others by posting on social media using #powerafterdv

Website: www.purposeafterdv.com
LinkedIn: https://www.linkedin.com/in/purposelawfirm/
Facebook: https://www.facebook.com/purposelawfirmaurora/
Instagram: https://www.instagram.com/purpose438/

Made in the USA
Columbia, SC
20 August 2024